Reticent Bodies

Reticent Bodies
Poems by Moez Surani

WOLSAK
& WYNN

Cover image: Daisuke Kunimatsu
Cover design: Rachel Rosen
Author's photograph: Arindam Photography
Typeset in Garamond
Printed by Coach House Books, Toronto, Canada

The publishers gratefully acknowledge the support of the Canada Council for the Arts, the Ontario Arts Council and the Book Publishing Industry Development Program (BPIDP) for their financial assistance.

The author gratefully acknowledges the support of the Ontario Arts Council.

Canadian Heritage Patrimoine canadien

ONTARIO ARTS COUNCIL
CONSEIL DES ARTS DE L'ONTARIO

The Canada Council | Le Conseil des Arts
for the Arts | du Canada

Wolsak and Wynn Publishers Ltd.
#102 69 Hughson Street North
Hamilton, ON
Canada L8R 1G5

Library and Archives Canada Cataloguing in Publication

Surani, Moez, 1979-
Reticent Bodies / Moez Surani.

Poems.
ISBN 978-1-894987-37-0

I. Title.

PS8637.U74R48 2009   C811'.6   C2009-904104-9

For my family

Reticent Bodies

6 REELS OF JOY

Kingston Poems

for James Lingwood and Carolyn Smart

THE CAPTAIN'S GARDEN

You are going to ask: and where are the lilacs?/ and the poppy petalled metaphysics?/
and the rain repeatedly spattering/ its words and drilling them full/
of apertures and birds?
                PABLO NERUDA

(i)

11:30 pm
Carry myself across the library
hold open his volume
read and reread
something revolving
as I revisit the line caught
in a pencilled circle and the tug
of a woman's adjoining scrawl

   This is what's happened to us

Back at my table
I neatly copy his lines
slowing my awful hand
so letters stand perfect
decent against his labour

              (ii)

              Neruda is disconsolate is
              splintered from her
              garrisoned in reticence
              his mind wanting no variegation of leaf
                   or sea
              no lyric ease of sound
              such luxury

              In his garden flowers stand rigid
              bleached of their opulence
              birds grown tired of their own songs

descend into fields of tall grass
swallow stones
push wet petals deep into throat
and so avoid the inquisition of wives

'A QUIET MAN'

Body expanding into bright rhythms
arms raised
carrying the amorphous billow
spine flinging this way
and that loosening
minute bones that
slept within neck

a shrieking lamp
dancing in New Delhi

Ankles flipping
like coins

Ankles snapping
like a shutter
            eyelid or
tip of pen releasing and

slamming back into case

---

*I have never suffered as much anguish and guilt over
missing a picture as when Thupten Nogdup poured
gasoline over himself and set himself on fire.*
EUGENE LOUIE, photographer

MAY STORM

All night

     blowing rain

suicidal acrobats
weaving through high branches

And Rilke
Je vais toujours travailler
Rilke advising solitude
advising immersion

Well I say
this is no way to live

SUNDAY MORNING (AFTER THE GUJARAT QUAKE)

This breakfast
having finished my coffee
I sit pinching the skin of an orange
watching the citrus firework in sunlight

My father tells me of a time in his past
He sat in the thirteenth floor
of a building he designed in Kenya
when the ground hiccupped and shifted

I picture him springing to his feet
to check the wall that is to absorb such tension.
Placing his palm against the tear in cement
the fissure he could slide his hips into
in a building that stood unharmed

This is how my parents' history is recovered:

        snapshots

                still frames

But what of all the darkness between poses?
Those blocks of time
when we are not smiling for some lens

        (I prepare once again to write about my father
        because his beauty is not apparent like my mother's.
        His is a dignity I believe to be sewn into his chin)

This man
who pins back blueprints
steps into them
identifying inefficiency
weakness of structure
This builder of tunnels and bridges

(How many times have I put off writing this
and even now as I begin
I know I'll tell only half-truths
of sunlight and not monsoon)

MY TRANSIT FRIEND

My transit friend,
how you comforted me.

You who lived as a primate in that jungle of personality
swinging and scaling those vines of conversation
in happy commute.

You held your belief that cars were elitist
and became the ascetic of transportation
losing yourself in that anarchy of culture and smells
evaluating shoes   skirts.

Our transit adventures:
bursting into song with others
who each held suspicious cups of coffee.

That time you cried out,
No, Iago, don't do it! You shouldn't incite him!
heads turned and you were gone
bursting out the rear door at a stop that was not our own
cursing the stunned man from beyond the glass shield
leaving me
in my basket of laughter.

And you,
the man who is often unseen in the corner of the room
hands dug in pockets, slouched in contemplation
perhaps still disconsolate over George shooting Lennie.

Well I saw you.
I saw your subtle gestures and learned to decode each one
the look at your shoes for disapproval
head at angle indicating an overstayed welcome
that wistful survey of ceiling, a craving for peppermint chocolate.

You didn't talk to me for days
when I told you there were no mountains in Ontario.

How I miss you now
my transient friend.

THE NECESSARY QUESTIONS

In a coffee shop south-west of Columbia University
two men are seated at the table to my left.
Between them, a manuscript inches thick.

- You enjoyed it?
- Yes, it was very funny.
- Did the humour fit the tone?
- Definitely.
- The humour didn't dwarf the characters? I was
  worried the humour dwarfed the characters.
- Oh, no. They rose above it.
- I was worried they would be conquered by the
  humour. The ending, did it surprise you?
- Her death? Yes, I was surprised.
- No, the orgy.
- The orgy was shocking.
- I wanted it to shock. I wanted it to be a shocking
  orgy. It didn't jar you though did it? I didn't want
  it to stun. I took great pains to foreshadow an
  orgy. I really loaded her dress.
- Yeah, the red dress.
- But did the orgy fit within the language of the piece?
  That's what's most important. Did it fit within the
  greater language of the piece?
- Oh yes. It was a well-nuanced orgy.

UNTITLED 1

What he loves
are her red polished nails

This remnant
from a night's dancing

And matching beads
that guard her neck

Is this
enough?

A love
for only

red polished nails
against the darkness of his arm

DESTRUCTION OF THE APPETITES

A destruction of the appetites
A world without mirrors
Erasing the self

In the caves of Lascaux
a galloping horse
in earth colours and mixed dyes

A concern for only the
dark mane and toughness of a hip
caught and etched red in mid-gallop

THE MISSING EXCHANGE

It has occurred to me
that Jane Austen persistently avoids
talk of massive erections dragged
like luggage through the house.

Among garden promenades
eternal courtships   planned laughter
there are no tentative questions
asked while gently fingering an earring.

No sudden pain
as prospects evolve
with a man
across the room.

No one pushed to drastic measures in the kitchen
cursing the oblivious paint
sink and faucet
pleading innocence . . .

There is never any rupture in the
manners that chain the air like
humidity. No
garden relief

after shoving glares.
The frantic couple
miming hallelujah
and cartwheeling off together.

What I am always hunting for
is the county nudist to stroll into the dinner party
into that white room of careful laughter

to take tea
white saucer   miniature cup
the room diverting its stare

and her turning
suddenly crying,
    "Why,

            isn't the garden lovely!"

And that reserved man
dragging himself from the kitchen
pulling free of his trousers
his pained whisper,

            "Yes, my love.
            I told you it was all in bloom."

SEVERAL IDIOMATIC DEMONSTRATIONS OF 'CARBUNCLE'

Somewhere near Clarington, the engine began to carbuncle.

He has strong forearms, an explosive bat – the
ball carbuncles off of it.

In my undergraduate Victorian literature class, the three successive
women-coming-of-age novels got some of us a bit carbuncled.

When she drinks too quickly she enters that familiar carbuncular sphere.

"Breaking up with me because you hold some sort of grudge against
women for original sin is ridiculous – it's a fucking myth – you get
angry for no particular reason and shut everyone out –" "Carbuncle,"
he muttered, leaving the room.

The President's speech was rife with carbuncle.

January leaves me carbuncled.

YARDSALING WITH ROBIN

Woke her at 7:30
my body trained
to trade sheets for shower
her laughter disbelief at my eagerness
for this Saturday morning experience
her mother and this town
swear by waves me off
to sleep ten more minutes so
I wake her again
and bully her into the shower.

Exploring this house of closets
stacked records and books
Why three copies of *Bleak House* I ask
O we don't have that book she tells me
her hair up in a damp knot

Yardsaling with Robin
yielded only this
soft poem,
a necklace of red beads
she bought for 50¢
to pull apart and reuse
in better aesthetic and the
sometimes kiss at red light

What the afternoon at Sandbanks
yielded was her best prank

I was sun tired
made a sand pillow
and while falling asleep
watched a seagull
huge he was
had Spain in that vast white belly
my head horizontal on the sand
so the bird stood odd sideways
indifferent to Newton's regulation

retreating and advancing
on me
Napoleon of the sands

I turned my head

sun tired
and kissed
your hip I love
your hips
Robin have
kissed them
how many times now
and drifted off

What she did
was warn me
that Napoleon
had neared my foot
and looked upset – No,
no, he's far, I mumbled, huge a definite threat
and I know what he's done to Sp—
and with her toe leaning over me
shocked me awake and she
she was in disarray in blonde curls of laughter

But now, the prank,
is inconsequential
really.

Evening and her
teeming sheaf of
hair over me
sometimes under me
reticent bodies
brought to riot
against each other
the incessant hip the

hip and loose
sand we each
know how
careful aesthetics
can mar these
elations

FICTIONS

ALLY DOLLE

Ally Dolle
moves slowly
room to room
when she is
without me.

Her face
taut as clothesline
burdened shoulders
body boiled so thin
body so long.

That summer her husband –
and she discovered
discovered Etta James.
Raised the volume
so it moved
room to room
with her.

Over and
over
          again.

Etta James.

Room
to room.

A sort of portrait:

Ally Dolle standing
crossing the room
away from me.
Leans her hand out window.
String of smoke rising,
curling above street.

Ally Dolle
moving slow
through room.
Leaves cigarette
to breathe
against window screen.
Hair still and yellow brown past shoulders
using hands to describe Spanish mountains.
Then twists her arm,
shows that spot
where foot slipped on wet rock
damaging her elbow.
Hands describing

(Ally Dolle
has an umbrella smile.)

groves of Spanish olives.

July night,
trying to sleep.

Torment of storm.
Rain like flung stones
against window against wall
window pane rattling mad between frame.

Cross the room in my underclothes
tear strips of newspaper
to wedge between glass and frame.

Sleep   torment   silent pane.

I used to say it. Used
to say it. Even
wrote it out.
Then
over and
over again
like a needle
tracing same section of groove
till ink crowded paper

(cus my veins got poison marching in it)

used to whisper,

"Oh Ally Dolle,
I'd never touch you"

But,

yellow summer dress.

And me,

leaping out windows.

Etta James and 12 bar blues
in a room made orange by sunset.

Beats stretch
like a body across mattress.

Beats long as

      as leg,

ankle to hip.

Melody like a thin white sheet.

All this parched skin,
and the appetite for water.

Come Ally Dolle,
time we swim.

Evenings meeting her
leaning against chain-link fence.
Walking those streets
amongst noise of bicycle chains
stop and start of cars
couples strolling, talking,
amongst metal braking of cars
then that seven-step drop into nightclub.

Nightclub like a smoke-filled mouth.
Standing at bar,
my pressed pants, pressed shirt
dance floor between us and band.
Man with large arms,
squeezing, swinging his cornet.
Ally Dolle
leaning
back against me,
my hand alive at her hip.

Song with bare shoulders
long legs

     (Ahh, Jesus)

wet guitar
the rough horn
wanting to break free, loose
and Eve's voice feeling it
waiting that half moment
gathering, waiting

     (Jesus, I'm there)

then stepping
and her voice leaping
over band spotlights
grabbing some lyric
and swinging it up, twisting
and tying it up on itself

up top at the street above
buildings, wires, traffic
before getting back
then that second leap from stage
across dance floor
band chasing her
like five wild dogs
and my hands alive
those seven steps below street.

Adding my weight
slowly to mattress.

Summer grip of heat
clinging to stark white walls.
August heat sleeping
in long white bones.

Speak slower, Ally Dolle.
Speak slow.

In that voice
more breath than whisper.

(Used to
say it.

   Over
and

     over again

like a needle tracing
same section of groove

       used to say
       "Oh Ally Dolle,
       I'd never touch you.")

Ally Dolle
moved slowly
room to room
when she was
without me.

WHITE TUB

Drive 2 ½ hours to see you
6 beers and enough clothes
the last 70 km drive slow
warned of deer and

meet you in the front yard.

Petalled skirt   your mother's plants
behind you exploding through windows.

Sleeping in your secluded room
waking every hour

to kiss your shoulder
or you mine.

The rain's fury
off your sloped roof
a continuous wet blade.

The plants retreat from the guillotine
and shriek

        summer delight.

Small tub.

The water cooling
before fresh heat
empties at my feet
is kicked to my hip
high tide
lose my arms
or gain them
lose my head
your discomfort
so I straighten up
kick the warmth
back up my waist
my weekday anger
ironed serene warm
water, breathing
against me.

Engine choked
by the previous night's rain.

Drive ten feet. Then another ten.
Restarting the engine. Drive back

the first ten feet. Then Picton, follow highway
that cuffs the lake to Kingston

to bring an absent friend a watermelon
that I conceal in a bed sheet

and is found days later
and celebrated with a call

that tells of a 2000 km move.

Some moods

cannot be re-visited with comedy
so they're left to accumulate.
Tableaux of grim mannequins
figures stunned from dialogue.

The knife carved into the watermelon
the flesh splitting bright as film.
Seeds dive laterally from the knife's discourse
the blade falling into sheets
that once held orgasms and repetition.

POEMS AGAINST ENGLAND

French poets are always forming groups and declaring war. They love principles, and above all they love fighting for them.
GLENN HUGHES,
Imagism & the Imagists

Because providence would not arrange things to suit his ideas, he was turning into a hypochondriac, would not even read the papers anymore, and roared with anger at the mere mention of England.
GUSTAVE FLAUBERT,
Sentimental Education

PACKING FOR MONTREAL

In the kitchen fruit basket the apples
wrapped in their red and green dirges
are upset that I am leaving.
They have been ignoring me.

Last night,
how quickly we moved apart.
A handshake, one friend ducking
into a cab that descended like an arrow
down Yonge Street.
We took another one north,
a handshake in my driveway.
With our different universities
we've done this
a hundred times.

Men departing without histrionics.

I leave only absurd
sentimental fruit behind.

NO GREAT LOSS

What wounds we inflict
the casual knives of conversation.
A tendency for the caustic
and the neurosis of the unrequited
released to street.

The leaves here have eyes send
rumours of self-destruction
the grim archive of roots.

Moscow Petersburg 'irrevocable'
littered throughout my translation.

Oblonsky,
something grand,
at the far end of a room pulling
diversions from his sleeves
juggling liquor bottles
improvising wild gossip
("Before she married me . . .")
affording the other end of the room
a moment's privacy.

Because the leaves here have eyes
spray messenger seeds into high winds
to report courtesies, the traffic of hands.

Vronsky went into the carriage
looking for his mother
and came out with Karenina.

Her brother's arm around her waist
laughter and welcomes in a Moscow station,
men throwing themselves into trains.

The crushed back
Vronsky's horse hauled away and shot,
neglected daughters,
    and one
hundred sessions of rushed love –

    scarves of perfume
    worn for the pleasure
    of Vronsky's embrace.

People slipping
into French.

Tant pis, he thought, feeling cold again.

Comfortable carriages.

–THE LAST POEM / I CAN REMEMBER WITH ANY–

What has happened
to Ondaatje's Vietnam poem that

image of a red sneaker
I vaguely remember my

latest dream the torso and shrieking
mouths of armless men Basquiat's

creations approaching my
clothed restaurant table their pitch

irritating my slim glass my slim date
attempting casual gestures but

intrusive torso shoulders blocking
conversation then falls with the cloth upset

-ing soup and maitre d' hand apologies
hauls away the exhausted

sack of hysteria and my girlfriend
that tender lyric my

heart and legs battering
my girlfriend awake what has happened

to that Vietnam poem that shoelace
resting timid against a breathing mine

REALPOLITIK

Since the death
of 500,000 Iraqis goes unmourned
so I will not mourn them
but will continue drinking to excess.

And though it has been written
that under the eternal threat of war
children gain anxiety disorders
and are found banging their head against floor and other available cement –
I will not mourn them.

I will not mourn the dying and deformed
because an idealist cannot be happy.
And I want to be happy.

So I will laugh and marry
and continue drinking to excess.

SMALL POEM

The R-535 bus
halting up
Parc Friday
evening drive home
crowd find a seat
my shoulder
against hers and
my leg too this
for me
is big
city intimacy

(THE LOWELL POEMS)

The Lowell poems I read softly to you over the phone – his wife's

incessant blue wave clapping over him. Wave and man

moving through each other without harm alteration

and the curled silver earrings you always seem to be wearing

how we could share this beer conversation nothing more

APOSTROPHE TO CANADA

Land of mighty lake and forest!
Where stern Winter's locks are hoarest;
Where warm Summer's leaf is greenest,
And old Winter's bite the keenest;
Where mild Autumn's leaf is searest
And her parting smile the –

ALEXANDER MCLACHLAN

hello, you.

COUNTRY OF THE BLUE

*. . . the gulf between the 'real world' and their own isolated,
imaginative selves often remained a conspicuous one or, on the
contrary, collapsed altogether and left them in the bluest of
countries, the country of American romance.*

ERIC J. SUNDQUIST

Late evening blackout
seizing work, aspiration
in its grip.

So cards and wine
in the candle's waver.

Between hands
standing before the kitchen window

the glazed snow
everywhere

holding full moon
in its expanse.

There were once men who observed logic in all this
who sat tranquil at a table like this one
pouring landscape into unblemished syntax
saw the woman they craved and encrypted her
quality into the bank's contour –
some could make the sonnet breathe!

or split the pomegranate   and stagger from its excess
    (a friend who cannot handle
     poets who imbibe wisdom from fruit)

So take the tone of unswerving devotion
the iambic heart   and sound proclamation
leave everything that squabbles.
The woman you love will leave the man she is with
if you can offer better carnival
or thrill her without skin let me
tell you about life

The Japanese restaurant on Parc
he realizes he is landlocked

He cannot swim and that vaults
to the top of his priorities ahead of marriage
reconciliations and getting a dog
which will be called The Governor
('He went for a walk with The Governor')

The conversation at times laboured. He pushes
the tumbler of cream away from his place setting.
He has been preoccupied absent-minded
if he tumbled into the cream and thrashed about

he would be disgraced welcome to
gallows humour the Country

of the Blue our wet
romantic tradition well
come

Drunk flights 1:30
after calling up an old friend, he rises

steadily into the hallway
needing a beer
to subdue this profundity

*"Was ist
Aufklärung?"* Bent over,
his head in the fridge.

Back in his room
savouring the foreign prosody.
Its recurrent music

Come home and
hang my head on a hook.

"is quiet. Let's be quiet. Let us listen:
– What for, Mr. Bones?
          – While he begins to have it out with Horace."

Miss Anne
throe pee.

Acoustic guitar on the floor and sometimes us
women on the couch upside down
look at you I say look at me she says
something in the room is red
my insides southern hemisphere Chris stands leaves
then I'm working a broom collecting these odd clear countries
into dustpan you look predatory she says
don't feel predatory I say her ankle came down
took the wine glass and spread it over the floor
earlier we were sharing dreams
Chris and I dreaming of car crashes
the women of grim pregnancy
see how we're gendered she says I say O
go home evening sleep partitioned neatly by nightmare

The branch   ordering the day's snow

Was ist
Aufklärung?   & rougher debates

over women   Bly
earning potential break down into coarse tongue
people who don't smoke lean away
thoughts return tempered

What will you be in
some years or rather where
tranquil evening recollection
who wants to go home
with you and who you'd like to go home with
beer bowls of popcorn

Is this what I wanted   when I came here?

The tree could go on creating complex
snow filigree if it likes but I am obtaining no metaphor insight
nor deriving wisdom   four months and

what I have done is march my intellect in moods
across the length of a dime and

sometimes though not lately am fine   with this breadth

NOCTURNE

Leaving the grocery bags on the table, I set

a red pot on the stove. I walk

round the dark apartment.

(WALKING HOME)

Walking home
across Pin up
Parc no bus the

only traffic rum
running in me
half singing when

shit I cursed a cat
leaped from cover
of leaves shit

shit I thought
and thought it was
over it was all

over. Fall night
good traffic
running in me.

6 Reels of Joy

MORNING
for Alessandro Porco

Spring. Back-
yard thaw.

Grass splitting
anxious through soil.

From the kitchen
collecting coffee
spreads its nerves past me
the smell of it
leaning with me against the wooden balcony rail
disrupting
birds

that rise
from fence

into noise
that is neither language   nor song

UNTITLED 2

I meet her in the driveway.

Hugging her in front of her car,
she asks if I can drive. Then, leaning

over the gear shift and parking brake,
hugs me again.

Grieving Clara.

LEONARD COHEN

After looking into his cereal spoon,
Leonard Cohen knocked over his chair. Backing away from the table,

he saw himself in the dense angle. Opening the cupboard, he saw himself
spread over curved metal soup tins.

THE DISSEMBLERS

2001. My mother and sister
travelling India together
gain reduced museum admission
by passing as citizens.

A guard stops them
and asks who the Prime Minister is.
Vajpayee! my sister answers.
And the Finance Minister?

Vajpayee, my mother tells him.
Name anyone in local politics.
The three of them laughing now.
Vajpayee, she insists.

GUY DE MAUPASSANT

Driving her fork
into the bowl
and pushing the damp
green into her mouth.

The other two talk.

Driving her fork
into wedges of red
inhales that with wine
so more is tilted. Her mouth
draining our table of its colour.

This morning, walking in the cold
I remembered the stark
letters I sent you.

And your letters
with the epigrams
that you sent me.

I wonder if you know how they tolled,
your careful epigrams, hours after I read them,
on my walks.

Then I remembered our walks on the cold boulevards
with the horseshit and the unhappy people
– and how in our long coats we ran after cats!

So I wanted to write to you
to let you know that I am feeling
big again, though nostalgic.
And that I wish, friend,
despite what you may think,
that we could be running
in our long coats again.

The cats here have become impudent. And this city,
I think, could use you.

The cold

driving us from streets to underheated
rooms where we make love over tablets.

Rolling
and rolling in
cones of sleep
after she undressed with drama
across the room removing her soft
blouse and returning from the closed door
so we could feed on sections of the other. Her heart

pivoting between the
attention of how many men.

HOW DO YOU IMAGINE THE FUTURE

Let us buy
a red boat,

you
& I,

and push it
into bluest water.

The colours will be elemental
('yellowest sunlight')

as will the
describers.

You can bring
your swimsuit.

And I will find a barbeque
and my loosest shirt.

Nights together, below
a popcorn moon?

How do you
imagine the future . . .

Let us buy
a red boat,

you
& I,

and push it
into bluest water.

A DEBT
for James & Chris & Rob

so much depends
upon

a red wheel
barrow

filled with
liquor

friends in the
yard.

QUIXOTE AT THE BAR

Tell Sancho Panza
that I will need ten more minutes here.

Tell him to piss against the fence
while he is waiting.

GUY DE MAUPASSANT (II)

*What, then, did Flaubert understand by beauty, in the art he
pursued with so much fervour, with so much self-command?
Let us hear a sympathetic commentator.*
WALTER PATER

I become Boswell around him.

I see him Sundays
when bark closes his face.

He is an unhappy planet disregard the
garrulity of his letters he is something
from Ovid becoming woman or lion
on whim becoming delusion
or child as the bark slams over his stomach
and we sit here complaining of the Paris snow.

I remove my eyes
from him. And he touches

my wrist from across the table.

Smiling, waving a fork.
"Tell me something," he says.

BASHO

(i)

Lying in bed
alone. Because

I asked
the other women
to leave.

(ii)

Were I to
lie against you
we would be forsaking
all this

land.

(iii)

The rain
and the rain and the
rain! Cottage weekend

four of us
in the kitchen
the watermelon the plum the mangos
– and still the rain!

(iv)

Since there
is no beer or wine
I drink brandy
and make
my face.

(v)

Journeying
to the garden
with a coffee. And moving
the chair from the sun.

(vi)

I like that we are
competing to write the
happiest poem. And not
because I am winning.

HAPPY TRAVEL

Flying

across Montreal on Jo's blue bike.
Westmount a blur. Working
up Cedar until the Côte-des-Neiges wa-

hooo!

        (not having
        to pedal)

Then working up Parc take Rachel
and I'm the swerving despot
of the eastbound bike lane turn up
that street east of St-Denis and walk it
across Mount-Royal haul it upstairs

to Jo

who laughing offers me water.
And her recent thrill
with Mr Barthes.

QUIXOTE, ROCINANTE, A PLAIN

                Reclined

on an almond.
There are

saucepans in the sky.

HAPPY KITES

> *no laughing matter:*
> *you must live with great seriousness*
> *like a squirrel*
> NAZIM HIKMET

Our life together will, I think, have a chasm.

Ten years. Twenty years. An insignificant chasm.

Our feet will visit countries
that haven't yet graced us.

My innocent feet.

You will send me your long letters
and I will phone you

before we
amble towards
each other in old age and fence
timidly with our canes.

We may age into reticence. And endure
the grieving of someone we love
so much.

And may begin measuring
our conversations. As though
what we have in us has, by the years,
been distilled

or poured
through black rocks –
griefs, joys, the hundreds

and hundreds of morning reflections
that our life affords us – and through those rocks
become sacred.

Joyous mornings
like this one

when you shared your ritual coffee with me
the coffee that you made each morning before
sitting down to your hyphenated and rhapsodic writing
crushing the heated milk into cream.

Or we may not become reticent.

And may leave
this world
happy kites.

Spilling our words and thoughts and cares haphazard and with joy.

We spoke through all of this
this morning after you woke me
from dream into that guest bedroom of yours
that was absurd with sunlight.

If what we are doing is practicing life
we are making headway here.

THE PATRIARCH'S LOVE SONG

Tonight if I cannot kiss you
I will pull apart my dinner plate in frustration.

My wives worry
missing my former humour
my large sons pulling me into rooms,
"We will find her."

> The clerics
> are withholding
> their services.

My daughters find my behaviour proper
commensurate with their ideals

and for my sake,
notable rakes
have subdued themselves   around you.

No one accepts my alms.

Lady
you have left

the whole town
grieving.

VACATION

(i)

Walking from Vedado, north through the cemetery San Cristóbal.
Small plants grow from the stone of graves.
Another grave smashed into, exposed,
a plant also growing there. Walking north

to the university, uphill, alongside Banyan trees
and their liquid roots that
continually pour into lawn
so that they are nearly jaywalking with us
to the grass island between double lanes of traffic.

Our first full day.
Sweating from standing and sweating
from sitting. The three-hour walk
past Marti's inscribed epigrams
now blocks from the Malecon,

Rob and I let the other two carry on
and laugh

as we inhale ice cream
that began draining over our hands
as it was passed to us.

(ii)

Our plan
the 7:15 Viazul morning bus ride
Havana to Trinidad.

Nearly missing the bus.
Because one of us
woke decided to masturbate
and went back to sleep.

(iii)

Crabs small as
coins shift this
way and that.

Stopping now and
then for water sun block
mutual complaints
about gears and uncomfortable seats.

The midday sunlight
narrowing us.

Our long bicycle ride

until I could pull the cool blue
blanket of water over me

and burst
from the heavy blue
to receive the slow orange flight
of Frisbee.

(iv)

4-5. The afternoon Cuban
storm. Blocks
of water

trap us under
a colonnade.

Drinking cans
of beer quietly. Happy

after our day's talkative walking.

(v)

Pleasantly

smashed in Viñales. At the table

beside us a man talks about
the Gobi because the Gobi
will impress her. Camels
are what he's banking on.

Camels camels
camels camels camels.

Camels.

(vi)

4-5. The afternoon Cuban
storm. Water stacking like crates.

Our day: Viñales, Pinar del Rio,
running through Havana. A woman with water
to her ankles. Our second-last day. Chris and I

running in the street the rain to Rosa's.

Acknowledgements

Thank you to Noelle Allen, Lindsay Hodder and the team at Wolsak and Wynn; to my editor, Jeanette Lynes, who soldiered on and delivered sensitive edits despite missing crucial keys from her keyboard; to Daisuke Kunimatsu for generously contributing his art; and to George Elliott Clarke, Steven Heighton and Mikhail Iossel for their guidance and support. Special thanks to Carolyn Smart for her help in arranging the manuscript and her years of friendship.

Early versions of these poems were initially published in *100 Poets Against the War*, *Arc Poetry Magazine*, *Carousel*, *Echolocation*, *Kiss Machine*, *Prairie Fire*, *PRISM International*, *Queen Street Quarterly*, *The Dublin Quarterly*, *The News International*, *Vallum* and *Versal*; thank you to those journals and their editors.

Poems Against England is for friends from Montreal. "Basho (iii)" is for friends at the Stinson cottage. Special thanks to Robin Heron for her indispensable help in the final stages of this book.

Moez Surani's writing has been included in numerous anthologies and literary journals including *Carousel*, *Prairie Fire*, *Vallum* and *Arc Poetry Magazine*. He has served as writer-in-residence for the Toronto Catholic School Board and curator for the Strong Words Reading Series in Toronto. He was the recipient of a 2008 Chalmers Arts Fellowship which supported a trip through India and East Africa.